LONGLEAF

LONGLEAF

poems

JOHN SAAD

GREEN WRITERS PRESS   *Brattleboro, Vermont*

Printed in the United States

10 9 8 7 6 5 4 3 2 1

Green Writers Press is a Vermont-based publisher whose mission is to spread a message of hope and renewal through the words and images we publish. Throughout we will adhere to our commitment to preserving and protecting the natural resources of the earth. To that end, a percentage of our proceeds will be donated to environmental activist groups. Green Writers Press gratefully acknowledges support from individual donors, friends, and readers to help support the environment and our publishing initiative.

Giving Voice to Writers Who Will Make the World a Better Place
Green Writers Press | Brattleboro, Vermont
www.greenwriterspress.com

ISBN: 978-0-9982604-4-0

COVER PHOTO: ALYSON SAAD

PRINTED ON PAPER WITH PULP THAT COMES FROM FSC-CERTIFIED FORESTS, MANAGED FORESTS THAT GUARANTEE RESPONSIBLE ENVIRONMENTAL, SOCIAL, AND ECONOMIC PRACTICES BY LIGHTNING. SOURCE ALL WOOD PRODUCT COMPONENTS USED IN BLACK & WHITE, STANDARD COLOR, OR SELECT COLOR PAPERBACK BOOKS, UTILIZING EITHER CREAM OR WHITE BOOKBLOCK PAPER, THAT ARE MANUFACTURED IN THE LAVERGNE, TENNESSEE PRODUCTION CENTER ARE SUSTAINABLE FORESTRY INITIATIVE® (SFI®) CERTIFIED SOURCING.

For Alyson

∾

ACKNOWLEDGMENTS

◌

Poems from this book first appeared in the following publications, and some have been revised:

ISLE: "Prescribed Fire," "Longleaf," "Bay Windows," "The Parthenon with Archeologists, 1837," and "Diamondback"
Birmingham Arts Journal: "Southbound"
Kudzu House Quarterly: "A Gutted Bird"
Steel Toe Review: "The Gulf of Mexico," "Karate in the Garage," and "The Sow-Taker"

"Southbound" was the state poetry winner of 2014 Hackney Literary Awards.

My sincerest thanks to the following friends, teachers, mentors, and editors for their devoted guidance and encouragement: Kerry Madden-Lunsford, M. David Hornbuckle, Kieran Quinlan, Gale Temple, Kyle Grimes, Jim & Tina Braziel,

Alison Chapman, Halley Cotton, Jason Walker, Cheyenne Taylor, Shelly Cato, Madison Jones, Myra Crawford, James Crews, and Dede Cummings.

But especially: Adam Vines, without whom these poems would not be possible.

CONTENTS

∾

PRESCRIBED FIRE   3

SOUTHBOUND   5

A GUTTED BIRD   6

AFTER GARDENING   8

"BENEATH ALL IS LAND"   9

THE LIMESTONE QUARRY   11

THE PARTHENON WITH ARCHEOLOGISTS, 1837   12

NO PLECTRUM   14

A LIVING NATIVITY   15

THE RECESS LINE   16

PUNISHMENT, BY MEANS OF STEVE MCQUEEN   18

SOLDIER   20

THE GULF OF MEXICO   22

THE RUT   24

CRATER LAKE   25

FIRELAND   27

EXODUS   29

BAY WINDOWS   31

LONGLEAF   33

KINDLING   35

THE FLOWERED SEPULCHER   36

SAFEGUARD   38

THE SOW-TAKER   39
PLAINSONG   41
DIAMONDBACK   43

LONGLEAF

PRESCRIBED FIRE

In everything there is something that must burn,
to purge what sap is left out from the heartwood,
and in this summer's flush a wet pine bog
is as good as any other stand we'll take.
Our hands are crazed from grubbing out sweetgums,
and wrists unbuttoned by pulaski swings.
Our driptorches blot brush with diesel flame,
penning the hardwoods in flanks, the greasy mire
squeezing our rubber boots around our ankles
with every step. The backfire slinks
through understory, sucking, then absent.
The longleaf bark papers and flits with coppered buckeyes—
disked bracken and milkwort flicker out in heaps,
and the varicose pitcher plants retort like flare
stacks before folding into the topkill.
"It's a fine servant, but a damn poor master,"
the fire boss warns us over a candling pitch
pine shoot. As it subsides into the slough,
he cants his yellow hard hat and bites off
a Red Man plug, gnashing with arms akimbo.
From the firebreak, the spark and slow ash resign
to proper execution, yet my tongue
is resin. Beside the break, in scrap, I find
a traveler pint unearthed by the Bush Hog's blade—
once someone's unction before limping home,
now chipped and glazed in mud like a tortoise shell,
its label no more than a weathered epitaph.
I bury it behind a cypress knee,
hidden as if a lie. The winds now shift:

the needles fall, the embers twitch, my eyes
give up their focus, and sweat from my brow seeps
like sap. Men, snake-like, shed their thermal coats
while others take axe and torch in hand.
The quivering corona of each hard hat
dissolves into the bog's pine splinter and crack—
the everything that has been burned,
the everything that will, and the fire in between.

SOUTHBOUND

On Route 5 down to Marion, a backroad
coughs up a logger dogclutching through a plume
of clay and shale: his smokestacks belching black,
slick pine poles staying the slewing iron bunk,
and red flags flailing like flushed crossbills.
His left mudflap hussy has lost her right
likeness, as if in a haggard fairy tale,
and gravel doveshots my Camaro's hood.
Scrapwood then caroms off the dimpled blacktop
into splintering midair pinwheels. I draft
behind the logger for miles, my left arm tanning
outside the window. The speakers spit with each rut—
young Iggy caterwauls about *the forgotten boy,*
the one who searches and destroys. We pass
soy fields and redbrick churches, satellite-
eared mobile homes neighboring scaffolded
white Revivals, and shacks swathed in vine like
shacks swathed in vine. We downshift a hill. Skid-
marks swerve the double yellow, then vanish.
In tall grass, off the shoulder, a woman stakes
checkered 3 flags around a tinseled cross
already overburdened with Crimson Tide logos.
This place is at a loss for words,
and our old sayings, if not dead, fall short—
unlike a pine pole through a windshield.

A GUTTED BIRD

With our Italian over-unders
and leather flasks of Ardbeg,
we GPS dogs point-frozen
on bobwhites in wiregrass.
The sandhill plantation plots
flush with coveys scatting
in skips, shots bursting at low
angles as hunting lines break down.
The dogs bay, the birds flip
from their crests, and the hunt
slips into the burnt-end sky
and marching pines.

         For half the meat,
Old Henry skins and guts those birds
for us beneath a turkey oak,
letting loose the latchkey under his tongue:
clipping a quail at the knee, he gabs
about family hogkillings; jerking
the craw out, how he brews his own
wine; a quick rinse, and his uncle
suffocated in a tar kiln. A gutted
bird rolls across the tabletop,
its flesh as clean and bright
as our best blaze vests.

         Old Henry
didn't pay a cent, but earned
this pine stand in bones.

And if we weren't so full
of our loose gentry-fried scat,
we'd catface a longleaf
and choke down the turpentine
without holding our noses
or piddling in our seersucker,
then bury ourselves in a spoil pile
near the Tombigbee paper mills.
Until then, we'll stalk the pages
of high-gloss magazines for scotch
reviews and lodges and sweet tea
recipes we can't think to make—
better to look at on the page, where
amber never melts to silt brown.

AFTER GARDENING

Night falls and over the fence children
    trampoline through clefts of floodlight.

I tipi the last cord of winter in the firepot
    and you curl me a glass of wine,

then cross your legs beside the pergola of roses.
    Tonight, rows on rows of fevered azaleas

shield the mulberry-stained fence
    from the afterthought of silk,

and the few stars above compete for light
    in the city's shallow red sky. Firelight

divides your thighs, the moondog grafts the crowns
    of sweetgum to walnut, and atoms

of cork float in wine like constellations
    without design.

But I am given to forgetting,
    until my fingers map your skin

down to your navel,
    where the earth is smaller than a scar.

"BENEATH ALL IS LAND"

*—from the Preamble to the REALTORS® Code of Ethics,
composed in 1924 by committee chairman, REALTOR®, and
Presbyterian minister, Arthur H. Barnhisel of Tacoma, Wash.*

Dried mud flakes from my school
uniform onto the office
carpet while I crack my knuckles,

now tender as the flatsedge
behind the gym where I punched
Wheeler Tamblyn for some peace—

twice in his back, once in my own
leg, and finally a shot
to his nose. So would today's

lecture be the lacquered *learn
to fly under the radar*
again, or something lean like

don't make my same mistakes, son?
Behind the recline of Dad's
leather high-back, the idle

computer screen scrolls the code
Beneath All is Land, over
and over, like a debtor's

chorus. He bickers with the phone
about wetlands mitigations
and schedules, his fingernails

flicking the gray edge
of his desktop's glass,
where a photo of myself

yellows beneath, unearthing
a child at a groundbreaking—
the boy, like the place, built to suit,

roughed over, formed and poured
to hold any land as all land.
But the bare branches reach out

like today's flatsedge—I'm wearing
a man's hard hat, doing
a man's work for the first time.

Looks like the mud won, he begins.

THE LIMESTONE QUARRY

The canebrake, when pressed, opens to cedar crags
shooting roots out the rocky steps daubed with vellum

redbud wings. The pit terraces and buckles, shags
of grass clouding stone down to the bedrock's sputum

pool, a static green mirror of talus and sough.
In the summer, the town boys dive through panes

to tag the sunken drill, corroded with gault-blue scuffs,
its tracks dug deep into the pool's runner lanes,

its cab inviting their breath, until one fails to grasp
the plumose remains of a patched jacket by the collar.

Now grackle streak and trill the quarry without lapse,
and the rain mantles striated block like a cobbler

apron. Sluicing over the cleft with shell and spine,
the silt backfills the need to keep rock and rain in kind.

THE PARTHENON WITH ARCHEOLOGISTS, 1837

> "Once I was tempted to knock off a corner and
> bring it home . . ."
> —JOHN LLOYD STEPHENS,
> from *Incidents of Travel in Greece,*
> *Turkey, Russia, and Poland*

Spring has but two hues held and one last prey:
we keep its view against the hammered sky,
Pentelic marble clutching the hill, veined
in graphite, and still shouldering the quarry's worth
when we arrive. The only sound's the wind
pecking at parapet walls. Inside, the rare
droplet of rock reflects like an icicle's crack
while the antechamber overfills with our boot
heels on the toothing limestone floor. We pass
the saucer eyes of statues long ago
devoured by echoes. Another draft comes in,
ferrying the last of winter through the shadows,
its source at the portico, and we stop to lounge
on friezes in the sun, where fallen myths
are hoofless, handless, and muttering to no one.

Bay laurel sprouts through mortared brick. I sweep
away the leaves and crumbs, then splay my rules
and plumbs, shining my scopes before I shoot a line
and pace the metes. The hill and slab keep firm
when underfoot, but we know their slopes have knees
that stay for something to stir them up again.
Another man, another measure. This swollen land
will someday push our pebbles out to sea.

From the outcrop's edge, the kneeling scholars pry
at temple pillars for bits like Kentucky ants
tearing the rib fat from my father's calf—
limbs tangled in old fence and within sight
of a neighbor's pond. The bluing scraps of day
marble the coming night behind a ridge,
and this hill palls with sandy light. When we
collect our tools, a current skims my nape
and an owl eclipses the capital above me,
a slow glissade and pivot, alighting in
the olive groves we trespassed outside Athens.
Reckoning soil, I shrink the squares through columns—
the orchards fade. Twilight subdues the margins.

Parnassus in the morning, but tonight
the harbor inns will provide us wine to soak
our bread. As we descend the hill, I note
a corner token chip of Doric design.
The sculpted ox-horns break free with ease:
a nugget of horn-tip and cornice surveyed
against the dilating pink moon. Too small
to blot, too large to pack, so cast into
a tidal pool—at once and again an eddy of light.

NO PLECTRUM

My guitar was lovely in its waist
when I left it on the riverbank
in duff. Each visit since, I shore
my ruin with its mossy chord.
Once trussed by hand with parlor grace,
the spruce top splits like a seed, and its grays
spore on the weathered lacquer's gold.
With rain, the neck gives up its bow,
tuning to some inhuman scale,
no longer pitched by a finger's skill.
I do not recognize the taut
decay that choirs with a fluent flock
of grackle tempering the sky.
No plectrum strikes. Yet the water's rise
sheds rosette rings of entropy,
the strings now prone to a sympathy
for shoals and the cutbank's slow refrains.
As if things are given to the shapes
around them, I forfeit my guitar
and hear the water's dark applause.

A LIVING NATIVITY

Cold coming tonight, yet we convene here in pea
coats and shawls, camera-ready. The old grouse of stiff knees

while the young, red-faced by cupcakes and Tang, lag
and writhe on asphalt. Like a new sweater's hangtag

left in the offering plate, the rented camel's musk awls
the dark. Then, spotlights on a manger. A round voice
    drawls

through tape flutter to deliver the distilled Advent.
Under palms, a tethered mule slurps water from a pan, bent

shepherds shrouded in bathrobes grip golf putters
as crooks, and all confirm the birth of a butter-

skinned baby doll. All stay their blocking but the mallet-
headed camel, gnashing thatch and eyeing florets

festooned around the punchbowl. Wise men spill gums and
    oils
in chafed beards, and mute cherubs pose like gargoyles

where the preacher parks his coupe by the transept
door. Each year this scene asks in earnest what we accept:

Joseph's shirt tag pokes out BLAKE scrawled in red,
and the Magi came from just beyond the storage shed.

THE RECESS LINE

We fall into place—jumpers and ties,
jumpers and ties. The old teacher palms
each head in line, *one, two, three . . . .*
I tuck my chin, and feel her nails digging in:

"John, what on earth is in your pockets?"
"Rocks, Mrs. Baltz." The truth is a fool's
instinct, and Mizz Balls has no tolerance
for geology. "John, empty your pockets

right now." The eyes of the line stick to me,
and the old painted dog cocks an eyebrow.
But I have as good a claim as any to clumps
of pale orbs, the claystone's dimples,

and the glazed spells of obsidian discs
cached in the slots of my black pennyloafers—
all found their way under oak filth and jungle-
gym shade. *Rocks have it made,* I thought. Buzzards

circled, so I slapped up at the sag of my chest
pocket, retching stones and dirt into the air,
the breeze dusting Mrs. Baltz, the line
unraveling to plaid pieces of jumpers and ties,

jumpers and ties, ducking the gravel rain.
With all settled, and my name now nothing
more than chalkdust on a blackboard,
I stretch my feet out from under my desk

to catch the obsidian shine regained.
Shifting a minute spectrum through black pupils,
I imagine myself a pupil to a cleaner
blackness, where color hinges on the angle.

PUNISHMENT, BY MEANS
OF STEVE MCQUEEN

Dad jumped from his blue La-Z-Boy and snatched
us by our skinny arms. "Now, I don't care
who did what or said shit. Y'all sit
on that couch, not say a word, and watch
this movie until I say leave." The tired man's
discipline. At least the belt came quick, a sprint
to the TV epic's marathon.
                                   Quiet—
William Holden was busting out of
a stalag in German darkness. Standby.
The Duke grit-eyed as Rooster Cogburn,
cocking back and cawing, *Fill your hands,*
you son of a bitch! before charging down
Robert Duvall in an aspen meadow.

But behind the plywood Zenith's flares
were Dad's shelves: his old Chamber
of Commerce awards, now geodesic
glass warts and bookends; and his John Wayne
collector's plate above his parents'
army portraits—his mother a nurse
and his father accepting a medal
in a sepia wasteland, maybe France.

Commercial break over. Back to Robert Redford
as Jeremiah Johnson, building a cabin
with his Flathead bride and mute son, fighting
off Crow in Utah's high country.
                              Dad's "You can go"
always caught me off guard. Only Steve McQueen
kept me seated as he escaped Nazis
on a stolen motorcycle, gunning
it through 70mm
of wide skies wide hills wide farms, clearing that first
wire fence with ease. But that second jump always
got me as it did McQueen. I never saw it
coming, and neither did my father—
to be tangled up in barb wire, eyes
flinching in the sun, destined for the cooler.

SOLDIER

Defensive end in high school
is nothing to running coke
in Tuscaloosa, you told me
with a corner-smile. We
drove by Bryant-Denny Stadium,
the lights arcing, even on
an empty spring night. You kept
me from an ass-beating
that night back home in Mobile,
when I was drunk and mouthing off
to bluebloods, just before you left
for Iraq. *The Marines will get*
my head right, you told me—
you told yourself.
Then you returned
months later, still smoking
Camels with that same
half-laugh, half-scowl,
still teasing yourself by
quietly sizing up others,
still testing my loyalty
about the night you whipped
my cousin's ass, the one who
played wideout for Bama
but never played. We drank vodka
all night at the Gulf, then dove off
some rich bastard's hardtop yacht
into the oily canal, your broad
shoulders carrying no pain,
no remorse,

like the news said you should,
like you knew you wouldn't.
And nothing was washed away.
Your forearms were slick stones,
now tattooed with lightning
bolts, *One for each rag*, you told
us. I knew then you wouldn't die
over there. Suddenly you left
again for Hawaii,
for another assignment.
Word got back you drank a fifth
and climbed the Pacific's ridge
to dive out past the breakers,
further and further, but none
were deep enough
until one drunken slip sent
your body crashing
into the rocks.
It took them hours to hoist
you from the ocean's lathe—
your bones seized up
and your voice scraped out,
like a chained-up dog
wincing under a house on block
piers. And because we refuse
to stomach the sight of a man
anything less than the monolith
we want him to be, we leave
you beneath the floorboards,
the withered shape of violence,
licking your joints in the day's
dust and darkness, almost
remembering how to swim.

THE GULF OF MEXICO

Last winter, we walked
the fumbled light of live oaks,
where saw palmetto spurs

the understory by
fingerbreadths, then, unable
to hold, issues forth

the beach. We sat
before a rooted
sun, regathering

our pace and the words
we lost in the sands
of ground teeth. I found

a moment when love
overfills a gull's shadow
before we call it shade:

your arms clasped around
your knees, your body
like curled confessions—

and I forgave the Gulf
its familiar strangeness,
a dream of home with rooms

you never knew existed.
But it's too much for
me now, the horizon's

great flicker. The naked
margins give rise in me
to draw back from myself—

from us—and hide in
the backwater pith,
the fluted boles of cypress,

a gull in the hem of dunegrass.

THE RUT

In the plywood shooting house, you're half-naked
in gooseflesh, and I'm just a blue-throated fence
lizard, hot-bladdered with whiskeyed coffee, baited
like deer on a salt block. Outside, a doe riffles quince

from the young rye while a buck charges behind.
She's sour-tongued, but he comes darker than a vow,
with piss-wet knees and a neck as swole as a fired pine.
The way the woods devote to death your eyes skin out—

my thumbnail's blacked in dove heart and harrow grease,
strumming your ribs before you drop me like
an onionskin to zero in. A piece
of ourselves will hang by its tendons later tonight,

a slurry of blood and cold pitch pooling beneath
the sawtooth's floodlight. The fresh jaw of our task
brought us this blade-thin night: the taste of your teeth,
a cartridge on my stomach—the flinch of cold brass.

CRATER LAKE

On the Devil's Backbone,
　　　a fellow hiker

snaps us on the rim, grinning
　　　like tubesock
　　　　　　idiots before

the heavy mantle of conifers
　　　and wrinkled
　　　　　　mirror of heaven.

The Klamaths called this place
　　　Mount Mazama,

before it was a rain-fed
　　　caldera on
　　　　　　the desert's

edge. They fasted and swam,
　　　and witnessed

its collapse, just as
　　　all domes collapse
　　　　　　in time.

For now, we'll pay
　　　the nominal fee,

drive the rim,
       and buy the T-shirt.

A few tall boys
       and my long-lens

lights on a talus holding
       summer snow,
              here where

the bucket list is
       the free man's
              vision quest.

FIRELAND

I wake
to the ferrous
howls
of valley dogs
and the plinks
of tin cans

on rebar
whirling in
wind beneath
the firs, where
come morning
goatsuckers

will boom
and peent above
the sword fern.
Two years,
two thousand
miles since

I watched
the long-legged
flames
skittering
across
the pineknot waters
of The Basin,

the cedar
fish camp
collapsing
into its pilings,
into our wake.
Tonight

the easy dying
of my camp
stove sounds
like a hand
crumpling
a paper bag.

Thin clouds
skate the jetstream,
and a red
taillight tracks
ant-like
across the darkness.

EXODUS

I-10 is a dark march
east, past the blowdowns
and the roadside cars.
Near Florida, the nimbus

of a gas station's lights
snuff out the pine ridge
behind and the stars
above. The cars weave

together like midges
on a stone archway,
waiting for the pumps
to open at dawn—

they are those who left
their homes after
the storm's flash and surge,
and the vacant exposure

of *nothing left*. Some
mass over cigarettes
and warm beer. Others
lie awake in cars,

their faces creased
in each other's arms,
bare feet propped
upon the dash—

and I'm the one who
slept wryneck in his bed
last night, here to
siphon my share like

a stunted organ-valve.
But if they travel
deep enough, certainly
the host of pines

will wick away
the nimble waters
and plot the way to grace
in flames. I'll receive

my gas and witness
before work, but their barb
of earth remains in foot
until the stations run dry.

BAY WINDOWS

The mirror above the mantle
turns dark, blisters, then dilates,
seeing everything at once and nothing

at all. Behind my likeness, keys hang
in a coffered door. The Black Forest
cuckoo still leans towards noon,

and a queen's rook hounds
a king
into a corner.

But whose mallard flies
on heart pine above
the bay windows?

Outside, the anvil sky
dissolves over the purple pulse
of switchgrass. Hooded mergansers
wrinkle the spoil's opal pond as needles
charge the ground around the wood-pile.

Through an aperture of pines,
the Tombigbee swells in silence,
brown water sculpting white bluffs,

rising, rising—

the dignity of witness, of the rains
finding gaps the dam cannot bear.
Here is a home that is not yet a home

until the river enters the bay windows.

LONGLEAF

The duff,
the fernspine

underfoot,
where light

coils
the crooks,

leaves
needledrift

on holes
and shells,

the shagged
blowdowns,

and scales
darting,

lithe,
crimping

early red—
say

a crowning
syllable

without
waste,

come March,
burning

candlegrass
into

a tendered
clearing.

KINDLING

The pleasure of a wood-pile's
in the stacking of shape and time,

like a handed-down stamp collection
or second-rate baseball cards,

a summer's moths pinned under glass
or a photo album with vacancy;

hell, even a friendship,
or stingy poems,

and the will to trust
the small ones—

all the things that never seem
to split quite right

and are never enough
to burn.

THE FLOWERED SEPULCHER

scrolls lilies and larkspur
  to a carnation dome

and rose spires. The priest's
  hands, wrapped in chains,

flourishes the censer's bells,
  while old men, chanting themselves

native, pluck a man
  from a tree. The painted

Byzantine faces, intoned,
  peeling gold leaf with a kiss,

hold fingers to their lips, as if
  shushing children in the aisles—

a girl palms a sliding puzzle
  in the afternoon blaze of stained

glass wings stooping on
  a concrete sill. And I remember

last fall's last hunt: the mosaic
  stubble of corn and sunflower,

persimmons still green on the branch.
  My thumb speared the belly

of a shot dove, prying
   free the lead-split chest.

Like a child tearing open
   a sponge in search of water,

I broke the bird's gut,
   spilling kernels of wheat

and goatweed onto the table's
   jigsaw of black blood and feathers.

I tried to thresh out a seed
   slotted in the table's furrow,

but my hands clustered with
   inky quills. The wind was so still

I felt my body bubble
   and drift in the bucket of raw

water and dove breasts, the chaff
   unwilling to soften and fall

from my hands. I landed, back pressed
   against a wrested heap of lead

shot, and above I saw the heart-
   shaped breasts sinking towards

me, the fell plumes of oily life
   floating on the water's surface.

SAFEGUARD

A bobcat shades
  slash pine
      along the firebreak—

the clap of my lever
turns her head.
      The shot
      opens
her breath

      then yearlings
spring from brush
only to disappear
  again

in the gray quick
  of last year's
      cutting.

THE SOW-TAKER

Winter scores the politics
of meat, when hunters bring hogs

to Mr. Spiller so his neighbors
might eat. "That old man has seen

the world and never left
these woods," they like to say,

as if one old man carrying
a greasy come-along

and a burrstone name can all
alone keep the woods, the hamlet,

hell, the state! Deep in the pines,
his winch and chains hang slack

as chimes from a magnolia's
bottom limbs, just above

a hoisting gall. The tree's backside
drops dried-up crescent gourds

and the braided blackness
of coachwhip skin. Tonight,

he's due a sow or two,
so he lolls in a nook

of naked roots, through half-sleep
and hiccupping winds, the night's

mobile of stars and a lowing
Tenn-Tom barge. Yet enough

awake to thumb through his lists,
pruning those that have passed,

he notes what names are next
and who still owes him from last spring.

PLAINSONG

"There's wildness in some wood lots that's extraordinary."
—JIM HARRISON

We used to hear about a tramp
who'd break into homes,
and dress himself in suits
and fix tall sandwiches
with the crusts cut off.
But is it breaking in if the doors
are unlocked? Cops thought so.
So did the housewives once
they'd come home to their sofas
sagging with a shaggy banker
eating salami on Iron Kids bread
while watching Sportscenter.
They'd scream, then out the back
he'd go, suit, sandwich, and all—
his daily taste of the good life.
Cops caught him living in the scrap
lot behind my house, under two
loblollies snaked in creeper vine.
Nothing but city critters in that lot,
and the occasional coyote whose belly
gets him hemmed in by the traffic.
The tramp—he'd built himself a shelter
in that lot from old fence and mimosa
limbs, covered it with a blue tarp
the cops saw once the leaves fell.
He told them his name was Plainsong,
and I watched as he was led away,

his hands cuffed, his arms kinked
by larger men. It's a wonder how
a man can live wild if you bother
to look. I know my pantry was full,
but with my doors locked and shades
pulled, he passed my home outright,
and I missed his neighborly break-in.

DIAMONDBACK

Just north, a dozer was felling trees in a slash.
The fragrant crack of cedar sounded close—
but not so close as the surging rattle just off
the road, beneath the shade of privet and pine.
Each day since Dad had moved us to the marsh,
my heels churned up the flatwoods' summer mesh:
the gator's slough, the osprey's quarry in
its claw, and the indigo's red-faced gloss at creekside.
But the diamondback's fat coil was still a myth
that slept in tortoise holes and basked alone
in asphalt heat, only revealed through death—
blackened by tread and sun, its patterns erased.
Yet here so near our home, a head concealed
itself in turns, its rattle poised and vowed,
its diamonds like a hundred open mouths.
Then cause arrived, and something in me lost
its footing between fear and home, urging
me back indoors for the .410 pump. Beyond
the iron bead, I traced its length through brush
until the eyes came clear. I fired and saw
behind the splash of earth that all was marred.
As if to claim myself a snake, I dragged
the headless sag onto the road in sun.
At the sound of gears, the yellow dozer appeared,
rounding the corner, led on foot by two
men sweating through their shirts. "You keeping it?"
the tall one asked. But no. "Take it," I said,
having no use for it besides a thing
that should be killed. The shorter man unsheathed

a knife and sliced the rattle off. He slid
it in his pocket, then slung the diamondback
into the dozer's bucket, one mangled end
of snake slumped over the toothing rim like a tip-
bit tongue. It puffed and dripped what all remained
as they backed out down the road, back to the slash
of privet and pine. Later, I followed their tracks
and watched them piling stumps and scratch for burn,
the loblolly crowns shaking the horizon
before they fell, the rattler nowhere
to be found. And there I shed the thought of myself,
that if I were any less a snake, I'd be more at home.

CPSIA information can be obtained
at www.ICGtesting.com
Printed in the USA
LVHW01s0907031217
558378LV00004B/12/P